POPULAR SONGS

HAL LEONARD
STUDENT PIANO LIBRARY

INTERMEDIATE PIANO SOLOS

Adele

T0055744

Arranged by Mona Rejino

ISBN 978-1-4950-6280-3

7777 W. BLUEMOUND RD. P.O. BOX 13819 MILWAUKEE, WI 53213

Visit Hal Leonard Online at
www.halleonard.com

From the Arranger

Arranging these eight solos of *Adele* has been an honor and a privilege. Her music is soulful and heartfelt, and she is a masterful storyteller. There is a certain poignancy that is always present in her music, and it allows for much freedom and expression on the part of the pianist. My hope is that your performance of these pieces will be as meaningful to you as the arranging of them has been for me.

Mona Rejino

An accomplished pianist, composer, arranger, and teacher, **Mona Rejino** maintains an independent piano studio in Carrollton, Texas. She also teaches privately at the Hockaday School and is a frequent adjudicator in the Dallas area. A member of *Who's Who of American Women*, Mona received her music degrees from West Texas State University and the University of North Texas. She and her husband, Richard, often present programs on a variety of topics for music teacher associations throughout Texas as well as nationally.

CONTENTS

Hello

Words and Music by Adele Adkins
and Greg Kurstin
Arranged by Mona Rejino

Moderately (♩ = 80)

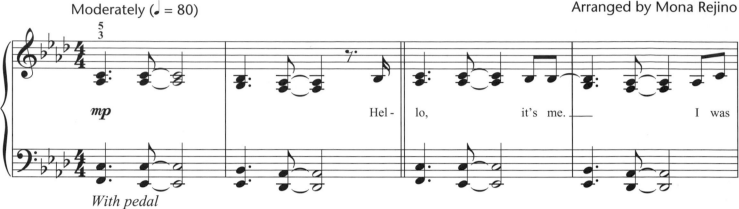

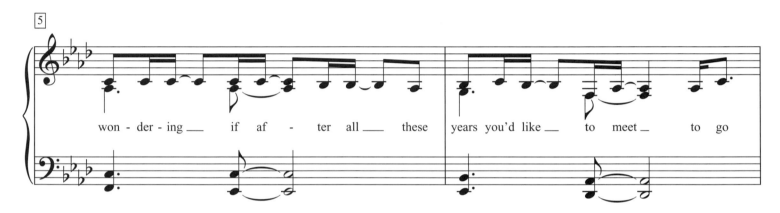

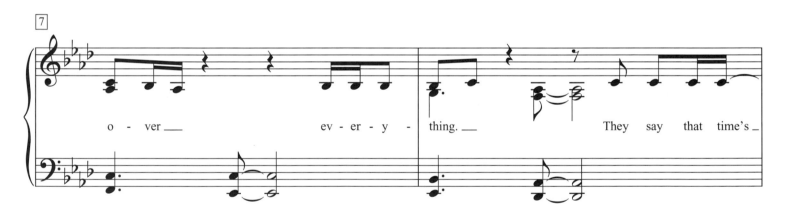

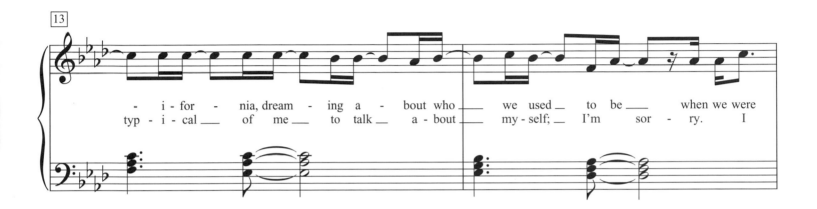

dif - f'rence ___ be - tween ___ us, _____ and a mil - li - on _____ miles. ___
se - cret ___ that the both of us _____ are run - ning out ___ of time. ___

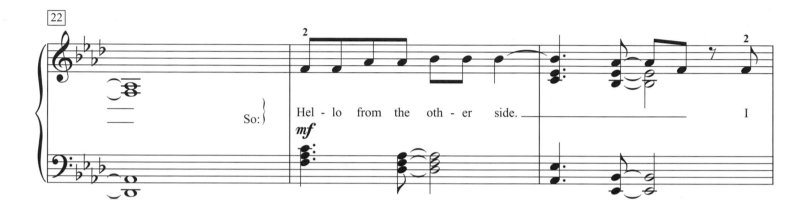

So: Hel - lo from the oth - er side. _____ I

must have called a thou-sand times _____ to tell you ___ I'm sor - ry ___ for ev-'ry-

thing that I've done, ___ but when I call, ___ you nev - er ___ seem to be home. ___

Hel - lo from the out - side. _____ At least I can say that I've tried _____

_____ to tell you ___ I'm sor - ry ___ for break-ing your heart. _ But it don't mat-

ter; it clear - ly ___ does-n't tear you a - part ___ an - y-more.

1.

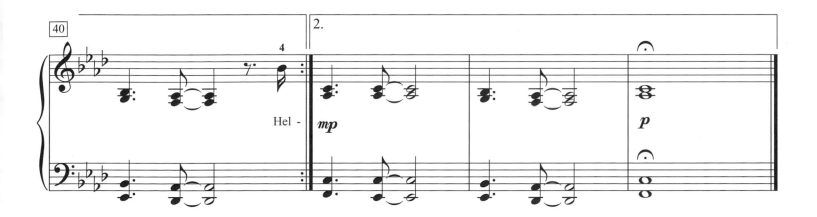

2.

Hel -

Million Years Ago

Words and Music by Adele Adkins
and Gregory Kurstin
Arranged by Mona Rejino

Moderately (♩ = 100)

mp

With pedal

I on-ly want - ed to have fun, ___
round all of the streets _

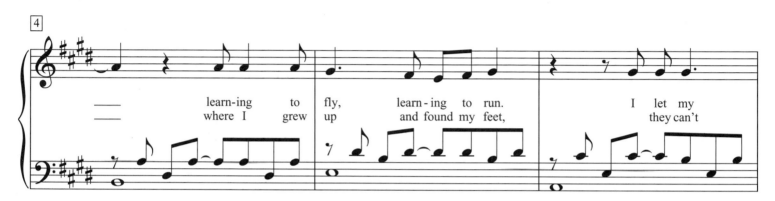

___ learn-ing to fly, learn-ing to run.
___ where I grew up and found my feet,

I let my
they can't

heart de - cide the way
look me in the eye,

when I was young.
it's like they're scared of me.

Deep down I try to
I must think

have al - ways known
of things to say,

that this would be
like a joke _

in — ev - i - ta - ble.
or a mem - o - ry.
To earn my stripes, I'd have to pay
But they don't rec - og - nize me now,

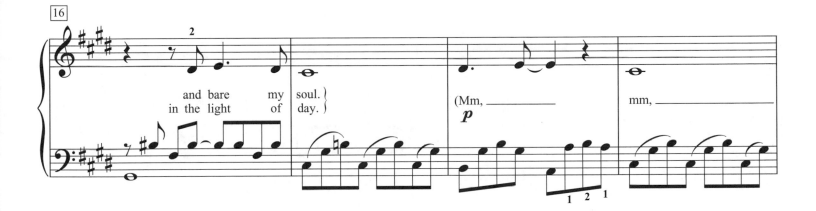

and bare my soul.
in the light of day.
(Mm,
mm,

mm,
mm.)

I know I'm not the on - ly one
who re - grets

the things they've done.⎯ Some-times I just feel it's on-ly me⎯

who can't stand the re - flec - tion that they see.⎯
who nev - er⎯ be - came who they thought they'd be.⎯ I wish I could

live a lit-tle more,⎯ look up to the sky, not⎯ just the floor.⎯ I feel like my

life is flash-ing by,⎯ and all I can do is watch and

cry. I miss the air, I miss my friends, I miss my moth-

-er; I miss it when life was a par - ty to be thrown,

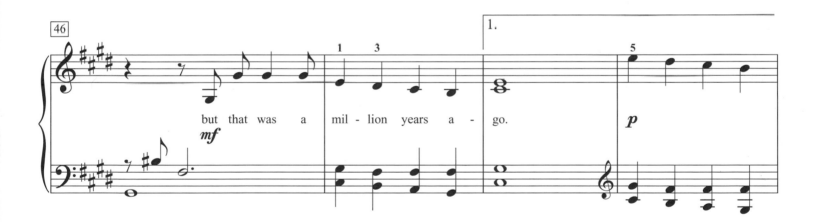

but that was a mil - lion years a - go.

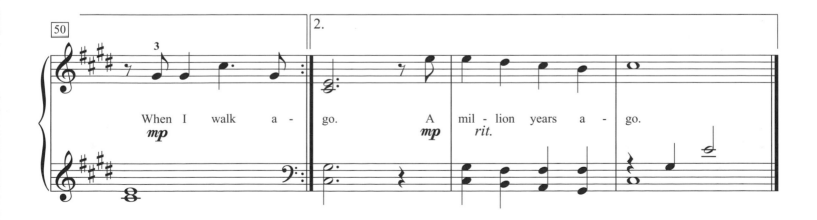

When I walk a - go. A mil - lion years a - go.

Make You Feel My Love

Words and Music by
Bob Dylan
Arranged by Mona Rejino

When the rain __ is blow-ing
When the eve - ning __ shad-ows and the

in your face __   and the whole world __ is   on your case, __
stars ap - pear, __   and there is no one there to   dry your tears, __

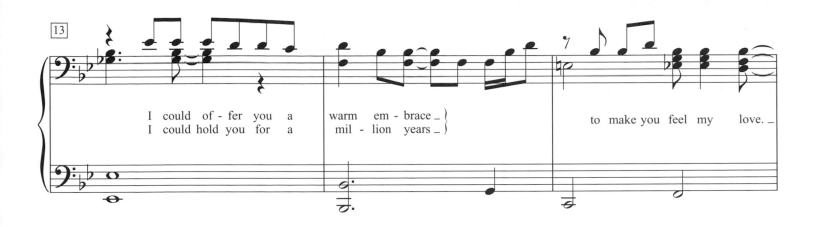

I could of-fer you a warm em-brace
I could hold you for a mil-lion years

to make you feel my love.

1.

2.

I know you have-n't made your

mind up yet, but I would nev - er do you wrong.

I've known it from the mo-ment that we met,

no doubt in my mind where you be - long.

mp I'd go hun - gry, I'd go

black and blue, ___

I'd go crawl - ing down the av - e - nue. ___

Know there's noth - ing that I would - n't do ___

to make you feel my love. _

f The storms are rag - ing on the roll - ing sea ___ and on the high-way of re -

gret. The winds of change are blow-ing wild and free; ___

you ain't seen noth-ing like me yet.

I can make you hap - py, make your

mp

dreams come true. ___

Noth - ing that I ___ would - n't do. ___

Go to the ends of the earth for you, ___

to make you feel my love, __

___

to make you feel my love.

rit.

Rolling in the Deep

Words and Music by Adele Adkins
and Paul Epworth
Arranged by Mona Rejino

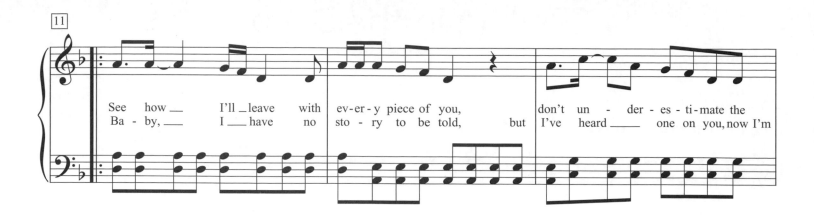

all. The scars of your _____ love, they leave me breath - less. I can't help

feel - ing we could have had it all. _____ Roll - ing in the

deep. _____ You had my heart in - side _____ of your hand, _

_____ simile

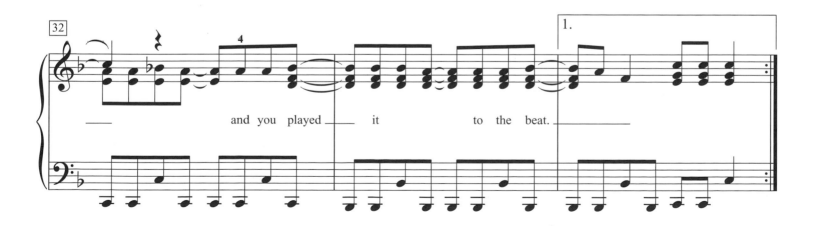

_____ and you played _____ it to the beat. _____

1.

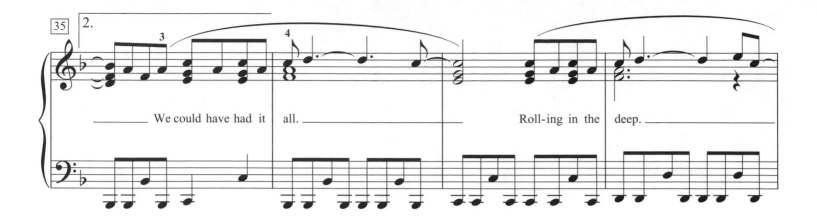

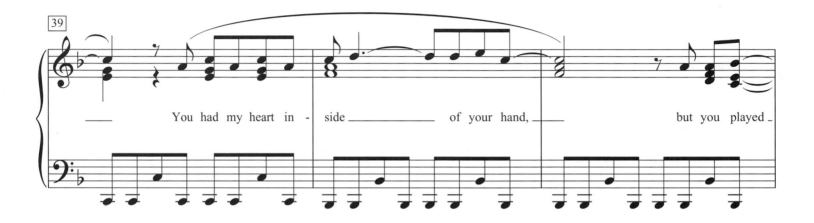

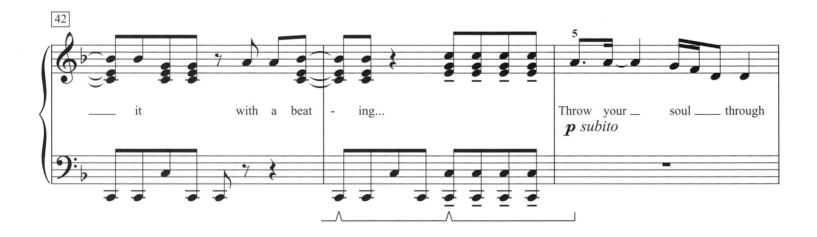

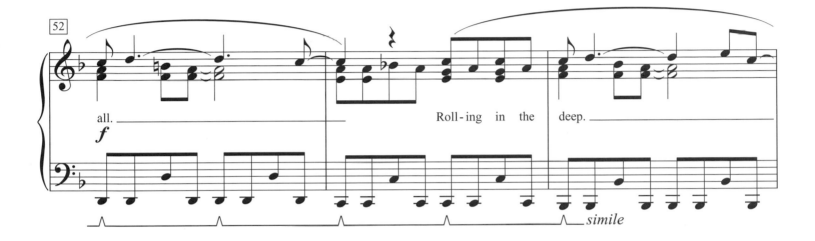

Someone Like You

Words and Music by Adele Adkins
and Dan Wilson
Arranged by Mona Rejino

hate to turn up ___ out of the blue un-in-vit-ed, but I ___ could-n't stay a-way, ___ I could-n't fight it. I had

hoped you'd see my face and that you'd be re-mind-ed that, for me, ___ it is-n't o - ver.

Nev - er mind, ___ I'll ___ find ___ some-one like

you. ___ I wish noth-ing but the best ___ for ___ you, ___

too. Don't for - get me, I beg. __ I __ re -

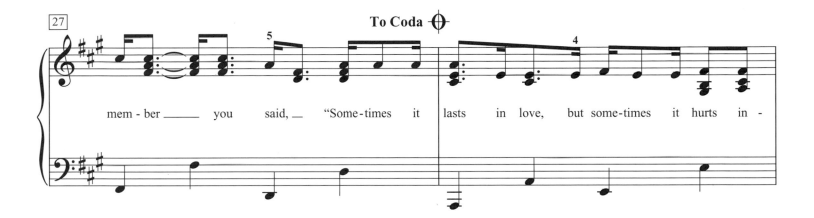

To Coda ⊕

mem - ber ____ you said, __ "Some-times it lasts in love, but some-times it hurts in -

stead." Some-times it lasts in love, but some-times it hurts in -

- stead. You know __ how the

mp

25

time flies, ___ on - ly yes - ter - day ___ was the

time of our lives. We ___ were born and raised ___ in a

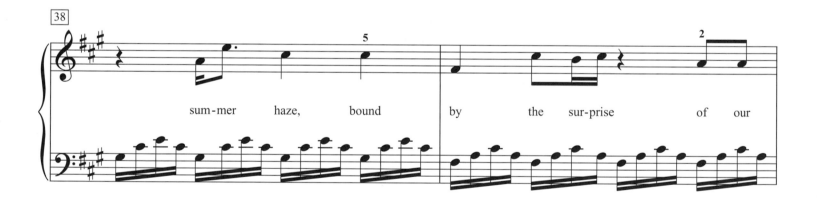

sum-mer haze, bound by the sur-prise of our

glo - ry ___ days. I hate to turn up ___ out of the blue un - in - vit- ed, but I ___

26

____ could-n't stay a - way, ___ I could-n't fight it. I had | hoped you'd see my face and that you'd be re-mind-ed that, for_

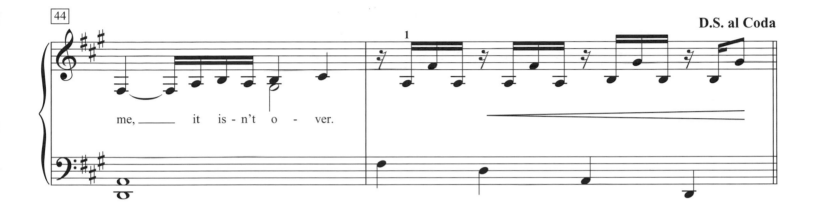

D.S. al Coda

_me, _____ it is - n't o - ver._

CODA

lasts in love, but some-times it hurts in - | stead."

Noth-ing com-pares, no wor-ries or cares, re - | grets and mis-takes, they're mem - o - ries made.

Who would have known how _____ bit - ter - sweet _____ this would

taste? *rit.*

mp *a tempo* Nev-er mind, _ I'll _ find _ some-one like _____

_____ you. _____ I wish noth - ing but _ the best _ for _ you. _

_____ Don't for - get me, I beg. _ I _ re -

f

mem - ber you said, _____ "Some-times it lasts in love, but some-times it hurts in -

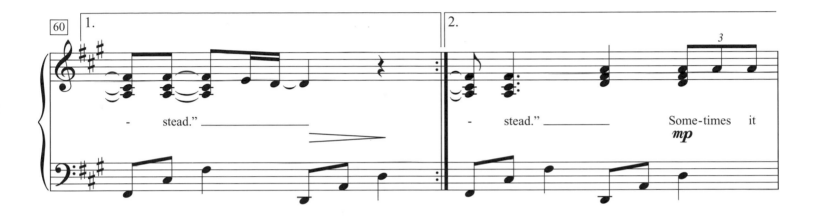

1.
- stead." _____

2.
- stead." _____ Some-times it

mp

lasts in love, but some-times it hurts in - stead. _____

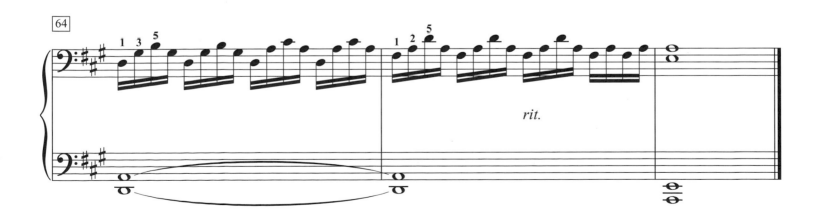

rit.

29

Take It All

Words and Music by Adele Adkins
and Francis Eg White
Arranged by Mona Rejino

Piano Ballad (♩ = 69)

With pedal

here.
this.   But go on and take it, _____ take it all _____ with you. _____

Don't look back _ at this crum-bl - ing _ fool. _ Just take it all ___ with my ____

_ love.   Take it all _____ with my _____ love.   May-be

_ love.   I will change   if I _____ must, ____   slow it down _

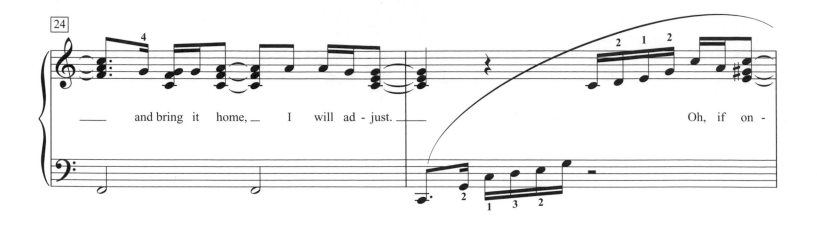

and bring it home,___ I will ad-just.___ Oh, if on-

-ly,_____ if on-ly you knew_____ that ev-'ry-thing I do is_____ for___

you.

mf

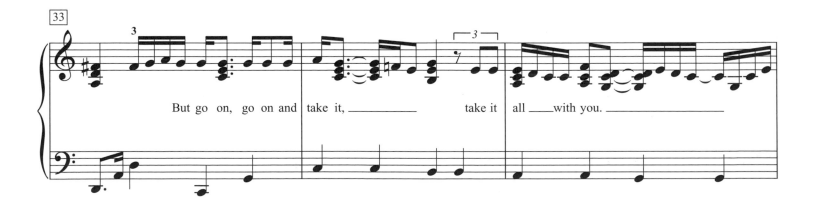

But go on, go on and take it,_____ take it all___with you._____

Don't look back __ at this crum-bl - ing __ fool. __ Just take it, _____ take it

all with __ you. __ Don't look back at this crum - bl - ing fool. Just

take it all with my _____ love. Take it all _____ with my __

love. Take it all _____ with my __ love. __

Turning Tables

Words and Music by Adele Adkins
and Ryan Tedder
Arranged by Mona Rejino

Moderate Ballad (♩ = 76)

mp

With pedal

Close e - nough to start a war,

all that I have is on the floor.

God on - ly knows what we're fight - ing for, all that I

say, you al - ways say more.

I can't keep up with your turn - ing ta - bles, un - der

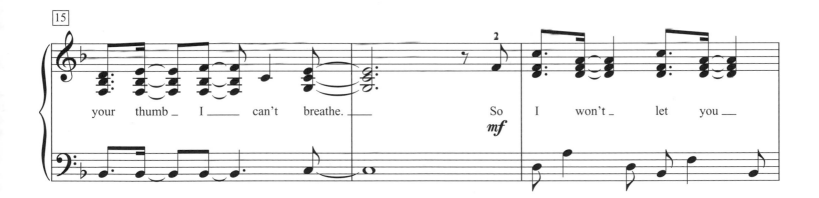

your thumb I can't breathe. So I won't let you

close e - nough to hurt me, no, I won't res - cue you just to de - sert me. I can't

give you　　　　the heart you think ＿ you gave ＿ me,　it's time to　say good - bye ＿

To Coda ⊕

＿ to turn-ing ta - bles,　　　　　to turn-ing ta -

mp

- bles. ＿＿＿＿＿＿＿＿＿＿　　Un - der hard - est guise ＿ I see, ＿

ooh, ＿＿＿ where love is lost, ＿ your ghost ＿ is found.

I braved a hun - dred storms _____ to leave _ you, _ as hard as you try, _

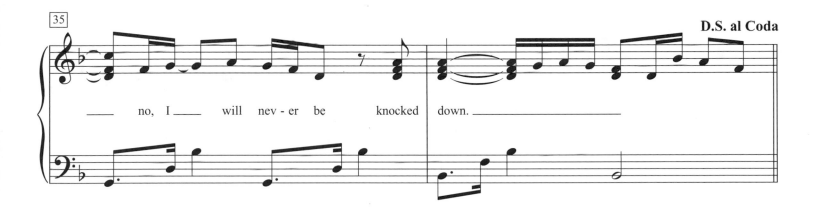

D.S. al Coda

_____ no, I _____ will nev - er be knocked down. _____

CODA

turn - ing ta - bles. _____

_____ Next time, _ I'll _ be brav - er, I'll be _ my _ own sav - ior

mf

when the thun - der calls _ for me. _

Next time, _ I'll _ be brav - er, I'll be _ my _ own sav - ior, stand - ing _ on my own _ two

feet. _ I won't _ let you _ close e - nough _ to hurt _ me, no, I _

_ won't _ res - cue _ you to just _ de - sert _ me. I can't give you the

heart you think __ you gave __ me, it's time to say good - bye _____ to turn-ing ta-

- bles, to turn-ing ta - bles.

Turn-ing __ ta-bles, yeah, __ yeah. _____ Turn-

- ing, oh. _____ *rit. e dim.*

When We Were Young

Words and Music by Adele Adkins
and Tobias Jesso Jr.
Arranged by Mona Rejino

But if by chance you're here a - lone,   can I have a mo-
I was so scared to face my fears   'cause no - bod - y told

- ment   be - fore I go? _____   'Cause I've been by my - self all night _
___ me   that you'd be here. _____   And I swear you moved o - ver -

___ long, _   hop - ing you're some - one _   I used to _ know.   You look like a mo -
- seas, _   that's what you ___ said,   when you left _ me.   You still look like a mo -

- vie,   you sound like a song, ___   my God, this re - minds _
- vie,   you still sound like a song, ___   my God, this re - minds _

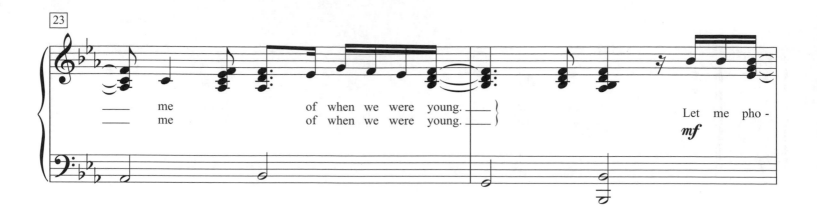

_____ me _____ of when we were young. _____
_____ me _____ of when we were young. _____

Let me pho-
_mf_

- to-graph you in _____ this light, in case _____ it is the last _____ time that we might _____

_____ be ex-act - ly like we were _____ be-fore we re-al-ized _____ we were sad _____

_____ of get-ting old, _____ it made us rest - less. _____

It was just like a mo-
_mp_

42

were there, ___ to when you were there. ___ And a part ___

___ of me keeps hold - ing on, just in case it has - n't gone, I guess I ___

___ still care. Do you still care? ___ It was just like a mo -

- vie, it was just like a song, ___ my God, this re - minds ___

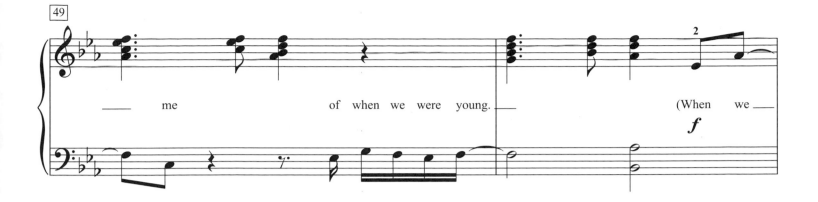

me — of when we were young. — (When we —

were young, — when we — were young, — when we —

were young, — when we — were young.) — Let me pho-

-to-graph you in — this light, in case — it is the last — time that we might —

be ex - act - ly like we were ___ be - fore we re - al - ized we were sad ___

___ of get - ting old, ___ it made us rest - less. ___ Oh, I'm so

mad, I'm get - ting old, ___ it makes me reck - less. ___ It was just like a mo -
mp

- vie, it was just like a song ___ when we were young.
rit.

POPULAR SONGS
HAL LEONARD STUDENT PIANO LIBRARY

The **Hal Leonard Student Piano Library** has great songs, and you will find all your favorites here: Disney classics, Broadway and movie favorites, and today's top hits. These graded collections are skillfully and imaginatively arranged for students and pianists at every level, from elementary solos with teacher accompaniments to sophisticated piano solos for the advancing pianist.

Adele
arr. Mona Rejino
Correlates with HLSPL Level 5
00159590..............................$12.99

The Beatles
arr. Eugénie Rocherolle
Correlates with HLSPL Level 5
00296649.............................$12.99

Irving Berlin Piano Duos
arr. Don Heitler and Jim Lyke
Correlates with HLSPL Level 5
00296838..............................$14.99

Broadway Favorites
arr. Phillip Keveren
Correlates with HLSPL Level 4
00279192..............................$12.99

Chart Hits
arr. Mona Rejino
Correlates with HLSPL Level 5
00296710..............................$8.99

Christmas at the Piano
arr. Lynda Lybeck-Robinson
Correlates with HLSPL Level 4
00298194..............................$12.99

Christmas Cheer
arr. Phillip Keveren
Correlates with HLSPL Level 4
00296616..............................$8.99

Classic Christmas Favorites
arr. Jennifer & Mike Watts
Correlates with HLSPL Level 5
00129582..............................$9.99

Christmas Time Is Here
arr. Eugénie Rocherolle
Correlates with HLSPL Level 5
00296614..............................$8.99

Classic Joplin Rags
arr. Fred Kern
Correlates with HLSPL Level 5
00296743..............................$9.99

Classical Pop – Lady Gaga Fugue & Other Pop Hits
arr. Giovanni Dettori
Correlates with HLSPL Level 5
00296921..............................$12.99

Contemporary Movie Hits
arr. by Carol Klose, Jennifer Linn and Wendy Stevens
Correlates with HLSPL Level 5
00296780..............................$8.99

Contemporary Pop Hits
arr. Wendy Stevens
Correlates with HLSPL Level 3
00296836..............................$8.99

Cool Pop
arr. Mona Rejino
Correlates with HLSPL Level 5
00360103..............................$12.99

Country Favorites
arr. Mona Rejino
Correlates with HLSPL Level 5
00296861..............................$9.99

Disney Favorites
arr. Phillip Keveren
Correlates with HLSPL Levels 3/4
00296647..............................$10.99

Disney Film Favorites
arr. Mona Rejino
Correlates with HLSPL Level 5
00296809 ....$10.99

Disney Piano Duets
arr. Jennifer & Mike Watts
Correlates with HLSPL Level 5
00113759..............................$13.99

Double Agent! Piano Duets
arr. Jeremy Siskind
Correlates with HLSPL Level 5
00121595..............................$12.99

Easy Christmas Duets
arr. Mona Rejino & Phillip Keveren
Correlates with HLSPL Levels 3/4
00237139..............................$9.99

Easy Disney Duets
arr. Jennifer and Mike Watts
Correlates with HLSPL Level 4
00243727..............................$12.99

Four Hands on Broadway
arr. Fred Kern
Correlates with HLSPL Level 5
00146177..............................$12.99

Frozen Piano Duets
arr. Mona Rejino
Correlates with HLSPL Levels 3/4
00144294..............................$12.99

Hip-Hop for Piano Solo
arr. Logan Evan Thomas
Correlates with HLSPL Level 5
00360950..............................$12.99

Jazz Hits for Piano Duet
arr. Jeremy Siskind
Correlates with HLSPL Level 5
00143248..............................$12.99

Elton John
arr. Carol Klose
Correlates with HLSPL Level 5
00296721..............................$10.99

Joplin Ragtime Duets
arr. Fred Kern
Correlates with HLSPL Level 5
00296771..............................$8.99

Movie Blockbusters
arr. Mona Rejino
Correlates with HLSPL Level 5
00232850..............................$10.99

The Nutcracker Suite
arr. Lynda Lybeck-Robinson
Correlates with HLSPL Levels 3/4
00147906..............................$8.99

Pop Hits for Piano Duet
arr. Jeremy Siskind
Correlates with HLSPL Level 5
00224734..............................$12.99

Sing to the King
arr. Phillip Keveren
Correlates with HLSPL Level 5
00296808..............................$8.99

Smash Hits
arr. Mona Rejino
Correlates with HLSPL Level 5
00284841..............................$10.99

Spooky Halloween Tunes
arr. Fred Kern
Correlates with HLSPL Levels 3/4
00121550..............................$9.99

Today's Hits
arr. Mona Rejino
Correlates with HLSPL Level 5
00296646..............................$9.99

Top Hits
arr. Jennifer and Mike Watts
Correlates with HLSPL Level 5
00296894..............................$10.99

Top Piano Ballads
arr. Jennifer Watts
Correlates with HLSPL Level 5
00197926..............................$10.99

Video Game Hits
arr. Mona Rejino
Correlates with HLSPL Level 4
00300310..............................$12.99

You Raise Me Up
arr. Deborah Brady
Correlates with HLSPL Level 2/3
00296576..............................$7.95

HAL•LEONARD®
7777 W. BLUEMOUND RD. P.O. BOX 13819 MILWAUKEE, WI 53213

Prices, contents and availability subject to change without notice. Prices may vary outside the U.S.

Visit our website at www.halleonard.com

0321
009